MW00916308

Thinking About Jail and Prison Ministry
A Guide For the Lay Volunteer

By Larry Nielsen

Cover Art and Graphics
by Laura Klumb

All scripture quotations are from the
King James Version of the Holy Bible.

ISBN: 1466270268

Printed by FBC Publications, Ft Pierce, Florida, USA

Dedication

This book is dedicated, with love,
to my wife and best friend, Teri.

Acknowledgements

I'd like to thank my pastor, Dr. William T. McConnell, for his support and inspiration, the Rev. Bud Jones for his evangelistic spirit, and my friends, Russell Griffith and Ken Johnson, for their encouragement and motivation. The true driving force behind this work is the Lord Jesus Christ, "For we preach not ourselves, but Christ Jesus, the Lord; and ourselves your servants for Jesus' sake."
II Corinthians 4:5

Introduction

Wisdom is the principle thing; therefore get wisdom:
and with all thy getting get understanding.
Proverbs 4:7

When I first felt the Lord's call on me to enter jail and prison ministry, I looked for some books on the subject. Since I was employed in a Christian bookstore at the time, I thought that finding some useful literature would be a piece of cake. It wasn't. I found some highly technical material for professional chaplains and counselors, but most of these were very secular in nature and not appropriate for a volunteer layman. I found biographies of famous prison chaplains and famous prisoners who had become Christians. I found doctoral theses and treatises on the relevancy and legality of faith-based prison programs.

What I didn't find was a simple book telling me how to bring the good news of Jesus Christ into jails and prisons. To paraphrase the old joke, they were telling me how to build a watch, when I just wanted the time of day.

What I wanted was a book that would give me information on the types of ministries I could do in jails and prisons. I needed to know how to get started. I needed to know what I would be allowed to do. I needed to know how to dress and who I could talk to. I needed to know how prisons "work" and who was in charge. I wanted to read about someone else's mistakes so I wouldn't have to make my own. I wanted to hear about some "real life" experiences from Christian volunteers and some testimonies from inmates whose lives had been affected by their ministries.

Introduction

What I wanted then is what I have written now. The title says it all. This is a simple guide for a person thinking about going into corrections ministry. This book begins with general information on jail and prison ministry, then focuses on the four major types of ministry for lay volunteers: worship team or bible study, visitation or lay chaplaincy, event ministries, and correspondence ministries.

I have gathered a number of testimonies from volunteers and inmates who have participated in all four types of ministries, and I have placed them in the text where appropriate.

The goal of this book is simple. I want a person thinking about entering this ministry to make an informed decision about whether this ministry is right for him or her. It is not a ministry for everyone, and I hope that reading this book will prevent someone from making the wrong decision.

I write about jail and prison ministry from a unique perspective; I spent a large part of my life putting people in jails and prisons. I came into this ministry after retiring from a long and successful law enforcement career.

I am not a "bleeding heart" or a prisoner's advocate. I have seen the blood, the misery, the cost in suffering and resources that these men and women have left in their wake. I also know that an encounter with Jesus Christ will do more to heal them than our justice system ever can. This is not just my belief, it is an established fact that you can read about in chapter one.

My training leads me to write in a straightforward manner, and my nature leads me to add humor. Do not let this belie the fact that when we minister in jails and prisons, we minister to some very dangerous people. People are in jail or prison for a reason. Some have violent tendencies and poor impulse control, and that makes for a very dangerous combination. This is a very small percentage of the population, but it is there and we must be ever mindful of it.

Take it from an old cop, "be ye therefore wise as serpents, and harmless as doves", and when in doubt, err on the side of the serpent.

I must add here, that almost all of my experience in corrections ministry has been in adult institutions. Volunteers thinking about working with juvenile offenders will find much useful information here but should bear in mind that ministry to youthful offenders will differ as much as any youth ministry differs from adult ministry.

I pray that what I have written will be of service to you. I know that there is no greater peace this side of heaven than to know God's will for your life, and I will be blessed if my work here helps you discover your ministry.

CHAPTER ONE

Why We Do What We Do

*Remember them that are in bonds as bound with them:
and them which suffer adversity, as being yourselves
also in the body.*
Hebrews 13:3

Dave had been talking for over an hour, his voice low, his gaze seldom moving from the desktop between us. We were in the chaplain's area of his pod in the south building of the justice center in Cincinnati.

I had met Dave the preceding Sunday when the church jail ministry team had conducted a worship service in this pod. At the end of the service, Dave had asked one of the members to pray with him personally. I joined in. When I offered a follow-up visit, Dave accepted. As a lay chaplain, I had visiting privileges throughout the system. I had called on Dave this evening, and he was telling me his story.

Dave had been born in Newport Kentucky, to a single mother who couldn't cope with Dave and his eleven brothers and sisters. Actually, they were half-brothers and sisters since each had a different father, and the fathers all had one thing in common: they had never been seen or heard from again. When he was about ten, the authorities lost interest in trying to keep Dave in school, and he was free to run the streets around the bars and strip joints of the Northern Kentucky of the 1970's (a mob-influenced area of corruption, much different than the progressive, respectable Northern Kentucky of today). Dave earned a little money by running errands and washing cars for the pimps and hustlers in the neighborhood.

One day, Dave noticed that some other kids his age always had a lot of money and never seemed to do anything to earn it. They were kids just like him, so Dave knew they weren't getting any money from their families. When Dave asked them about it, one of the boys took Dave into his confidence.

"You ever notice men, alone in cars, driving slowly around the neighborhood?" asked Dave's companion. With that question, Dave was introduced into the underworld of male child prostitution, a world that would steal his childhood and mold his adult life.

As Dave told me about this part of his life, I struggled to keep a poker face. Inwardly, I was amazed. I had worked with offenders for almost thirty years, and this was the first time a man ever made this admission to me. I knew then that Dave was "for real" and very deeply hurting.

When he was about 15, Dave outgrew the perverted desires of the men who cruised for boys, but not being able to support himself with his own body wouldn't be a problem for long. For the past couple of years Dave had been studying the pimps who controlled the streetwalking girls in his neighborhood. Dave figured that he could do as well as any of them, and he was right. A handsome boy with bright blue eyes and wavy red hair, he naturally attracted girls; and with the expertise for deception gained as a boy prostitute, Dave was quickly living well off the "earnings" of two or three girls.

But Dave wanted more, and the big operators weren't going to let a punk like him get a "stable" of more than two or three girls. So Dave moved on, into the heroin racket; heroin being the drug of choice at that time. An established dealer took Dave on as an apprentice. Dave would "hold" for his boss and make deliveries. It didn't take Dave long to learn to use the drug to manipulate people, and soon he had his string of girls back, now addicted, hooking for him, stealing for him and pushing for him.

Dave was riding high, living like a prince. At age 18, he had an apartment, girls, a sharp new car, a party every night, a thriving drug business and cash, cash and more cash.

Then Dave became his own best customer, and his world collapsed around him.

When he first got into the heroin business, Dave began "chipping" and "skin popping", using enough to get a mild high, but not enough to get hooked. At least that's what he told himself. Before long, he was hopelessly addicted. The drug took over his life, and when the money was gone, the friends, the girls and the parties went away with it. Dave began a twenty- year stretch of street life. He was now one of the junkies that he had once bled dry, living on the streets or off older women, shoplifting and rolling drunks to survive and buy heroin. It was a life frequently punctuated by jail and prison terms on both sides of the river.

Chapter One

Dave had told me about the hell of heroin addiction. "With other drugs," he said, "you feel OK, then you take the drug to feel better. With heroin, you take the drug to feel OK, because the rest of the time you're sick."

Now, at age 38, Dave was doing 180 days for shoplifting groceries. Ironically, Dave had never been arrested for a drug offense, only for crimes to support his habit. Consequently, he had never been sentenced to drug rehabilitation.

His tale told, Dave lifted his head and looked me full in the face. Tears ran from his piercing blue eyes; he sighed heavily.

"I'm 38 years old," he said. "I've got nothing. No home, no job, no wife, nothing. I've got a daughter somewhere who's better off without me. I've got nothing that a man my age should have, nothing. I'm tired of it. It's like I've never even been here, never lived. Now I've had my share of mission meals, and I said what they wanted me to say and prayed what they wanted me to pray to get fed, but it never really meant anything to me. But when you were here Sunday, your friend got my attention talking about Jesus. But I just can't believe its real, I can't believe it's for me. I'd like to believe it, and I'd like to have whatever it is that you guys have, but I don't know... If I could believe it, if you could make it real for me, I could go on, but I've got to tell you, man, I'm tired; just tired of this life and I'm thinking about checking out."

I was stunned. The man staring at me across the desk through tears had just told me he was about to choose Jesus or suicide, and I was the one who had to convince him that Jesus was the way. My mind raced, trying to think and pray at the same time. How would I do this?

Well, I've told you quite a bit about the man across the desk, now I should tell you something about the man on this side of the desk.

As far back as I can remember I'd wanted to be a police officer. In 1973, about the time Dave started running the streets, I was sworn in as a patrol officer for the Hamilton County, Ohio, Sheriff Patrol. In the following 28 years I served as training officer, traffic safety specialist, sergeant-squad commander, lieutenant-district commander, academy commander, bomb squad commander, and captain-patrol section commander. Along the way, I picked up the Greater Cincinnati Chamber of Commerce Police Officer of the Year award, and the Buckeye State Sheriff's Association Award for Valor, along with numerous other decorations and commendations. I write this not to glorify myself but to emphasize that I strove to be more than a cop; I was a cop's cop, a hardcase who believed that the saddest sight in the world was an empty jail cell. I had achieved everything that I could in my career, but I was an empty man, a man who didn't know Jesus.

Born and raised in the Roman Catholic tradition, I left the church as a teenager and only returned for periodic rituals like weddings, baptisms and funerals. Fortunately, our God is a loving and wise God, and in the years that I ran from Him, His prevenient grace was working in my life. He put my wife, Teri, in my life during those years, and our loving relationship is what kept me whole and sane in those heathen years.

Chapter One

Toward the end of my career I became very restless, noting that every award, every promotion, every assignment had left me unsatisfied, wanting a little more, hungry for something else. I finally realized that what I was missing was God.

Teri and I started attending a large non-denominational church in Cincinnati. I took the Alpha class there, and I was saved during that class.

I began to feel a strong pull on my life to do something different, to step out in faith and accept a new challenge. At that time, the retirement law changed and I became eligible. I retired and began seeking God's will for my life. I tried fishing in the Florida Keys, but sadly, that wasn't it.

I filled my days volunteering at the church and working part-time at a Christian bookstore. One day at church an acquaintance asked me how I could be there during the day when most people work. I explained about my retirement from the Sheriff's Office and we had a pleasant conversation. As I was leaving, she said, "You know, we have a jail ministry here, and they could use someone with your background." I smiled politely and said I'd think about it. I was really thinking, "Not in this lifetime, lady!"

About a week later, I was assisting a customer at the bookstore. He looked familiar, and we both thought we knew each other. We finally got it: he was the Rev. Jack Marsh, who had ridden with me occasionally as a police chaplain. He was now head of the justice chaplaincy in Cincinnati. We caught up on old times and, as he was leaving, he asked me where I attended church. When I told him, he said, "You ought to consider getting into their jail ministry." I thought this was an odd coincidence, and I also thought, "You've got to be kidding!"

A few days later, I was helping a customer select a bible. This time he was a complete stranger. We talked for about ten minutes about bible versions, books, prayer and other topics. After he had selected a suitable bible, we shook hands and he headed for the checkout. After taking about two steps, he turned, looked, me in the eye and said, "You'd be a good man to be in jail ministry." Then he walked away.

I knew from the Alpha program that God sometimes uses other people to convey His messages. I had been told three times in two weeks by three different people—an acquaintance, a friend, and a stranger—to go into jail ministry. I knew then that not only was God speaking to me, He was being pretty insistent. I surrendered at that point, reasoning that if God really wanted me in jail, the next person speaking to me about it could be a judge. Or He could have a big fish vomit me up on the courthouse steps, and I've seen some people who looked and smelled like that's exactly how they got there.

I got into the jail ministry despite my reluctance. A short time later I had a very profound experience with the Holy Spirit through the word of God that convinced me that this, indeed, is the ministry God planned for me.

After two years in the jail ministry at that church, God led Teri and I to become members of First Christian Church of Harrison, Ohio, and with the assistance of the pastor, Dr. William McConnell, I established a jail ministry team. During that process I also became a lay jail chaplain and

Chapter One

started a correspondence ministry to inmates all over the country. After years of ministering to inmates, seeing how they walk, talk and look, I'm now convinced that the third man—the complete stranger—was an ex -con who had been saved in prison. Who else would see that potential in me, and who better for God to use to give that final push?

Well, let's get back to Dave. After recognizing the nature of the challenge presented to me, I said a quick prayer, took a deep breath and started talking. I'd like to tell you that Dave accepted Christ that night; he didn't. But he didn't try to kill himself either.

You see, Dave didn't accept Christ that night because I didn't even tell him about Christ that night. But I did tell him how an 80-year old fugitive from a murder charge named Moses, living in hiding, became one of the greatest leaders of men in history. I told him how an orphaned Jewish girl named Esther became queen of Babylon and saved her people from extinction. I told him about a scared farm boy named Gideon, who led a small group of soldiers to a glorious victory over a mighty army. I told him about a prostitute in Jericho named Rahab, who put her faith in action. Then I showed him her name in the genealogy of the King of Kings.

I told him that when Jesus was ready to begin His ministry and needed disciples, He didn't go to the temple and recruit priests; He went down to the docks and got some fishermen. Then He pulled a guy named Matthew out of the tax rackets. I told Dave that God knows every one of us. He told the prophet Jeremiah, "Before I formed ye in the belly, I knew ye." The big news that God uses ordinary people, broken people, sinners, hardcases, and people like Dave, me and you is the second greatest story in scripture. And if Dave wanted to hear the greatest story in scripture, he would just have to come back for a second session.

You see, when someone is as lost as Dave, he doesn't even know he needs to be saved; but he does know that he has a terrible longing to belong to something, to fit into something, to be connected to something bigger than him. So Dave came back; and he came back again, and a third time. Then, during our fourth session together, Dave got on his knees, said the sinner's prayer, and accepted Jesus Christ as his personal savior.

That would be a good enough story if it ended there, but that wasn't the end. Dave still had 90 days to go and he knew he still had an addiction. He knew now that he didn't have to fight it alone, he had the power of the Holy Spirit on his side. Dave filed a motion to be transferred to a drug rehab program—about a one in a thousand chance considering his record—and miraculously the judge granted it. Dave was given the choice between a 90-day secular program and a 180-day faith based program. Without any coaching from me, being led by the Holy Spirit, Dave chose the 180-day program, even though this meant that he was essentially starting over his 180-day sentence from scratch.

Dave was given work to do in the rehab center. He attended classes about his addiction and did a lot of bible study. A man who had never held a job was now doing 16-hour days, six days a week.

Dave got his GED and even attended some college classes. He followed all the rules, did more than what was expected of him, and got strong and healthy. When his 180 days were up, the center offered Dave a job, supervising residents in the shop where donated items are cleaned and repaired. This was Dave's first legal, paying job. He took more classes and kept going to bible study. He started helping in the counseling groups and took classes in drug and alcohol counseling. Now Dave helps men find their way out of the life in which he was once trapped.

II Corinthians 5:17 reads, "Therefore if any man be in Christ, he is a new creature: old things are passed away; behold all things are become new." Dave is a new man, with a new life. John 11:25 reads, "...I am the resurrection and the life: he that believeth in me, though he were dead, yet shall he live:.."

When our worship team encountered him, Dave was a dead man; spiritually, morally, and emotionally, Dave was as dead as Lazarus. Jesus brought Dave back to life as surely as he raised Lazarus.

Now, is Dave an unusual success? Absolutely! For every Dave there are hundreds that we don't reach or that don't accept the gospel message when they hear it. It has to be that way; Jesus told us it would be. Not all of our seed will fall on fertile ground. But I know this: none of our seed falls on fertile ground if we don't cast it. It bears no fruit in our pockets. Can anyone say that reaping one Dave isn't worth the effort of sowing hundreds of seeds?

In the United States alone there are currently 2.3 million men, women and children in prisons, jails and juvenile detention facilities. Almost all of them have two things in common: they are right where they should be, and they need the saving power of Jesus Christ to heal them so that they can live in peace and dignity in the company of their fellow man. A handful of dedicated but overworked and understaffed professional chaplains can't do it all. Legions of lay volunteers are necessary to supplement their efforts.

Barna research indicates that 75% of released inmates will commit another crime and be returned to custody. However, only 14% of inmates involved in a regular, organized study of the bible will return to prison. As a retired law enforcement officer, I find that statistic staggering. Recidivism reduced by 61%! Think of the savings of lives, injuries, suffering and trauma! Look at the money saved by our communities, courts and governments. Think of the human potential not locked away, rotting in storage, but contributing to society, being mothers and fathers, church members, employees and citizens.

Lay volunteers have an opportunity to serve both their God and their country in jail and prison ministry. In succeeding chapters I will describe four ways in which this ministry can be performed, one of which can be done without leaving the security of your home. Adult men and women of all ages and levels of spiritual maturity can participate in these ministries, and all of them will be changed by their participation. Consider the following testimony from a volunteer.

Why Did You Come?

It was during one of my first trips to the jail when an inmate asked me an interesting question, "Why did you come?" His name was Martin; we had finished the worship service and had a little bit of time to talk.

Chapter One

Funny he should ask that, I thought, I had been wondering that myself. When I first heard about the opportunity to be part of a jail ministry, I knew I wanted to do it. It seemed like I could reach out to people who really need God. Yeah, we all need God, I know, but folks stuck in jail don't have the same opportunities to worship Him that I have. That's why I signed up.

That's not what I told Martin, though. You see, I had already been to jail with the ministry a couple of times, so I began to have more reasons. God's word tells us to visit people in jail. It doesn't get more direct than that, does it? I also knew someone that had been in and out of trouble and it seemed that God wanted me to do this ministry.

I thought more about the question, "Why did you come?"

I told Martin, "I came because God wants you to know that He loves you."

I didn't plan for that to be my answer, although I had tried to plan for an answer ahead of time. I just opened my mouth and those words came out. God loves everyone; I was just lucky enough to be the one He used to tell Martin.

Kirk Hopkins

Before describing our various ministries, I will explore in the next chapter the peculiar nature of the location of our ministry.

CHAPTER TWO

Incarceration Nation: Our Mission Field

Fear thou not; for I am with thee; be not dismayed; for I am thy God: I will strengthen thee; yea I will help thee; yea I will uphold thee with the right hand of my Righteousness.
Isaiah 41:10

Like a missionary to foreign lands, the Christian volunteer going into a correctional facility is entering a foreign land, a land with different customs, different culture, and a different government. Like a foreign missionary, the Christian volunteer must be aware of those differences to be effective.

The most important of these differences is the form of government. Jails and prisons are absolute dictatorships with a very narrow agenda. Regulations are numerous and penalties are swift and severe. We must remember that the goal of the facility is to confine offenders in a secure and humane manner, providing the necessities of life: nutrition, shelter, clothing, safety and medical treatment. We have no absolute constitutional right to minister in correctional facilities; we are permitted to be there, guests of the administration, subject to the rules of the facility. Our ministry is secondary to the goals of the institution. We do not dictate to the administration, we minister when the administration allows, where the administration allows, in the

21

manner the administration allows. Some institutions will be very liberal about ministry, some will be very rigid. All will have regulations we must follow, and failure to do so will almost always result in the termination of the ministry privilege for the person or team involved.

At a prison event in Madison, Indiana, I served with a man who had been involved in a similar event in Florida. An inmate asked him for his wristwatch. The volunteer had not familiarized himself with the rules of the institution, and he gave his watch to the inmate. Corrections staff discovered this breach of regulations, and the volunteer was banned from ministry in all Florida state institutions for life. This may seem unduly severe for a first offense, and an unintentional one at that, but we must expect that kind of consequence. We must always remember that facility staff members know more about running a prison than we do, and rules that seem arbitrary to us are quite logical in context of prison culture. Every rule and regulation is the product of a situation that detracted from the efficient operation of the institution. If ministry teams are searched prior to entry, it's because someone on a ministry team has brought contraband into the institution. Security philosophy dictates that what has happened before will happen again. Submit to the search without complaint and be glad that all volunteers haven't been banned from the institution.

Again, while inmates have a constitutional right to practice their religion, there is no obligation for correctional facilities to permit volunteers into the facilities. You have no absolute right to be there. In fact, we are standing on the very edge of the separation between church and state, and we could be one supreme court decision away from oblivion. Obey the rules, serve with humility, and treat the staff with respect and courtesy and you will be able to bring the gospel to the imprisoned. That's a great reward for a little submission. Remember 1 Peter 2:13, "Submit yourselves to every ordinance of man for the Lord's sake ..."

Many years ago, my late father supervised the power plant of a large Midwestern hospital. Noticing the expertise and familiarity with the equipment shown by a new employee, my father asked him where he had learned the trade. The new hire replied that he had just been released from prison and had worked in the power plant there. This surprised my father, because he knew that it was the hospital's policy not to hire people with criminal records.

About a week later the personnel manager asked my father about the performance of the new man. My father answered, "He does a good job, knows the work and gets along with the other employees, but I'm a little surprised that you hired him since he's been in prison."

"IN P-P-PRISON!..." sputtered the personnel manager, "that lying son-of-a-gun told me he was incarcerated!"

Words are important, and we must know some of the basic language of the criminal justice system to operate efficiently in that world. For example, the terms "jail" and "prison" are sometimes used interchangeably in general society. In fact, jails and prisons are two very distinct entities, each offering its own ministry challenges and opportunities.

A prison is a facility for long-term custody of persons convicted of serious crimes. Prisons have educational and rehabilitative programs and work details to occupy the inmate's time. With a lower turnover rate than jails, prisons offer good opportunities for long-term discipleship and bible study programs, as well as worship ministry. In most cases, prisons will have a larger population than jails, and more volunteers are required to sustain ministry.

A jail primarily provides pre-trial custody for persons who are accused of crimes and can't, or are not permitted, to post bail. Secondarily, persons convicted of minor crimes are sentenced to jail custody for up to two years. Unlike prisons, most jails have very few educational or work programs, and inmates pass the time with TV, cards and reading. Since the turnover rate is high, jail ministry focuses on short-term programs. The average stay in the jail system that I serve is six weeks.

A detention center can be either a jail or a prison, but this term is most frequently used for juvenile facilities. There are very few long-term juvenile facilities, generally only one per state. Most juvenile facilities serve as both a jail and a prison, and all have educational programs. The goal of the juvenile justice system is to return the child to his home as soon as possible, considering the safety of the community and the child.

Parole is a supervised release from prison prior to the actual duration of the term of imprisonment. Parolees who violate the conditions of parole are returned to prison to serve the full duration of the term.

Probation is a supervised release in lieu of prison. Probationers who fail to conform to the conditions of probation are sent to jail or prison to serve the original term of confinement.

Protective Custody, or "PC", is an area of a jail or prison occupied by inmates who must be protected from the general population of the facility. Informants, public officials, police officers, child abusers and persons convicted of particularly bizarre crimes are candidates for Protective Custody.

The Isolation Unit, sometimes called "the hole" or "ice" is a part of the facility where inmates who have violated the rules are kept for periods of solitary confinement.

The Keep Away List is a database kept by the facility administration which is used to regulate associations between prisoners. Inmates who are known enemies, codefendants, rival gang leaders, escape conspirators, or any other group of inmates whose association is detrimental to the safe and efficient operation of the institution will be on the Keep Away List. Lay volunteers organizing group bible studies or other activities involving multiple inmates must be aware that the Keep Away List will regulate inmate attendance.

Every jail and prison will have its own language and slang. Some volunteers will try to assimilate that slang into their own language in an attempt to create a feeling of familiarity with the inmates or in an attempt to appear to be an "old hand" at jail and prison ministry. This is a particularly bad idea. Volunteers who try this almost always make fools of themselves and lose credibility. Just be yourself. Inmates will respect that more than any attempt to assimilate their culture.

25

Chapter Two

Some slang terms are universal, however, and you should expect to hear them in conversation with inmates.

"Cellie" means cellmate.

A "kite" is a form used by an inmate to make a request. Many institutions require an inmate to submit a "kite" to see a chaplain or take part in religious services. Most of the inmates and staff that I've asked believe that the derivation of the term "kite" comes from "see if it will fly".

Many inmates will refer to a chaplain or any religious worker as "padre", regardless of denomination. This is actually a term of respect, so if you feel the need to correct the inmate, do so gently.

Christian workers should also remember that they have their own slang and language. We should never expect that inmates will understand "christianese" and we must keep our teaching direct and simple. There will be more on this in succeeding chapters.

In order to help the Christian worker stay safe and effective in the jail and prison ministry, I have developed the following list of ten guidelines. The six "dos", two "don'ts" and two "nevers" are useful in any correctional ministry setting, and were developed by researching the mistakes made by Christian volunteers through the years. The foolish person repeats his mistakes, the intelligent person learns from his own mistakes, and the wise person learns from other people's mistakes. This is an opportunity to attain wisdom.

The first "do"
Always Remember Where You Are.

When I was a young man I worked for a construction company. On one job, I watched ironworkers gracefully negotiate the spindly superstructure of a building high above the ground. At lunch that day I asked one of them how they had the nerve to work at that height. The old veteran became deadly serious, held his hands up in front of me, thrust one in my face and said, "this hand's for the company;" then showing me the other, said, "this hand's for me".

That was the fundamental fact of life for working in the sky. The fundamental fact of life in jail and prison ministry is that you are among some very dangerous people and you must always remember that always. Not all inmates are dangerous; in fact, very few are. But in most circumstances, you won't know which are and which aren't. And even if you do know, you want to minister to everyone, regardless of the nature of their offense.

When your ministry is going well, when people are learning, worshipping, growing, and giving their lives to Jesus, it's easy to succumb to euphoria and not recognize that maybe things are going too well to be true. We can't give one hand to Jesus and keep one for ourselves, but we can remember to remain objective about what's going on around us, and be discerning about the motives of those to whom we minister.

Some inmates may respond to your ministry in order to "butter you up" and gain your confidence so they can attempt to get you to break the rules by bringing in contraband, taking letters out of the institution for them or making phone calls for them. Some inmates thrive on controversy and chaos and may try to get you into a compromising position to discredit you just for sport.

Always keep in mind that things may not be as they seem. Be covered in prayer before entering the institution and during your time there.

"Do" number two
Be Aware of All Regulations and Support the Staff

Make it a point to know all the rules that apply to your ministry and, if possible, get a copy of the inmate's handbook and familiarize yourself with all the rules. Make sure you know what staff expects of you. Be there on time and leave when your time is up. Don't make the staff ask you to leave.

If an inmate complains to you about the institution, its policies, or specific staff members, refer the inmate to the grievance procedure. Be sympathetic without agreeing with the inmate. You don't know the whole story and arbitration is not your job. Jails and prisons are small worlds and if you say something against the institution or a staff member, it will get around and become known by the administration. Stick to the spiritual, and let someone else handle worldly matters. Always be courteous and humble with staff members, and look for opportunities to minister to them, too.

"Do" number three
Stay Within Sight of Other Volunteers or Staff

Privacy is a scarce commodity in a jail or prison, and an inmate may want to get you into a corner or behind a pillar to tell you something he doesn't want anybody to overhear. Don't take that chance. Always stay within sight of someone you know you can trust. This is both for your physical safety and to avoid any appearance of impropriety

"Do" number four
Dress Appropriately

Most facilities will have regulations regarding dress for visitors. There are three considerations regarding dress: safety, modesty and culture. Dress will be discussed at length in the chapter on worship ministry.

"Do" number five Know
Your Limitations

Inmates will pour out their problems to you and you will want to have solutions for them. Unless you are a counseling professional you may bite off more than you can chew. Remember why you are there. If you are there to teach, then teach. If you are there to pray, then pray. Don't be too prideful to refer the inmate to a professional, or even a more experienced volunteer. Don't think that you have to have all the answers, and recognize that a lifetime of poor choices can't be overcome in a day. You can always suggest prayer and help the inmate develop a better prayer life. That prayer life will be the foundation for further professional treatment.

Also, be aware that an inmate's "head knowledge" of the bible may be far superior to yours. I once ministered with an ex-inmate who had been "locked down" 23 hours a day for four years with nothing to read but the bible. His familiarity with scripture was unsurpassed, but the trip from his head to his heart took many years.

"Do" number six
Keep Physical Contact to a Minimum

Most institutions have rules which strictly define acceptable inmate-to-inmate contact and staff-to-inmate contact. Don't expect those rules to be waived for Christian workers. Handshakes are generally permitted, and brief hugs may be allowed. Holding hands during prayer is usually acceptable. Always make the contact brief and disengage quickly.

"Don't" number one
Don't Give Anything to an Inmate

Inmates may ask for money, postage stamps or food. Most institutions consider these things contraband. You may be able to give away bibles, tracts, or other Christian literature, but always check with the staff first because items may have to be examined before distribution.

Several years ago I was involved in a Christmas worship program at a juvenile detention facility. Unknown to the rest of the team, one of the volunteers had purchased a number of pendants with a cross made of nails. At the end of this volunteer's part of the service, he held up one of the pendants and said, "before we leave, I'm going to give each of you one of these...if it's okay with the staff."

It wasn't. Where he saw a cross on a string, the staff, appropriately, saw a mini-dagger on a garrote. Not only did he disappoint the children by offering something that he could not give, he made the staff the "bad guys" by asking about the pendants in front of the children. His actions embarrassed everyone on the team and staff and changed the whole atmosphere of the celebration.

"Don't" Number two
Don't Do for an Inmate what the Inmate Can Do for Himself

Most inmates have access to phones that make "collect only" calls. Inmates will frequently ask you to make calls for them from the "outside". This is because the number he wants you to call has a "block" on it. There's a reason for that. The person at that number doesn't want to hear from the inmate. In fact, there may be a protection order forbidding the inmate to contact that person. If so, by calling that person on behalf of the inmate, you may be facilitating the commission of a crime.

Inmates may also want you to contact attorneys for them, complaining that they haven't heard from the attorney in weeks, months, etc. It's not your ministry to be the liaison between the inmate and his counsel, and counsel will not appreciate hearing from you.

Don't carry anything out of the institution for the inmate. He may be trying to get rid of contraband prior to a shakedown (search of cells) or get a letter out past the censors. Just don't do it. There can be no legitimate reason for an inmate to ask you to do this.

"Never" number one
Never Do Extended One-on-One Ministry with an Inmate

31

Chapter Two

of the Opposite Gender

Many inmates come from a background where acts of kindness are rare, and they may misinterpret your intentions. A mentoring relationship may become more than just that in the imagination of the inmate. This is true in correspondence ministry as well as in face-to-face ministry. Opposite gender relationships are always a source of temptation, in prison or out, and we must take precautions to avoid compromising situations.

In I Thessalonians 5:22, Paul cautions us to "Abstain from all appearance of evil." Even in short-term ministry situations, you should always be within sight and sound of another team member when ministering to the opposite gender. At the time of this writing, there is a significant increase in the numbers of female inmates, and female ministry volunteers are in great demand.

"Never" number two
Never Intervene in a Physical Confrontation
Between Inmates

Overcrowding, boredom and stress inevitably lead to fights, and you may be in the vicinity of a fight between inmates. The staff is trained to handle these incidents. When you become involved, you risk injury and get in the way of the staff, preventing them from stopping the fight in the most efficient manner. You should also be aware that the situation may not be what it seems. It may be a diversion to draw staff's attention away from something else, or a feigned fight staged by non-Christians to disrupt your ministry. In any case, bring the incident to the attention of the staff and don't become involved in physical altercations.

The physical appearance of jails and prisons will vary from dungeon-esque to ultramodern; from the piled-up cell blocks of the 1930's to the no-bar "pod" designs of the late twentieth century. One prison that I serve would look like a community college, if it wasn't surrounded by razor ribbon.

As Christian volunteers, our concern is the population, not the architecture. The next chapter will address the focus of our ministry-the inmate.

One Volunteer's First Visit

"I wasn't sure what to expect on my first jail ministry visit. I had never been in jail before, although there are things I did in my younger days that could have brought me there. I had some fear and reservation before going. Realistically, I knew that first ministry experience would play a pivotal role in deciding whether or not I would be back for more. I remember the "clank" of the door locking behind me that day. That was the sound of freedom being lost. It was a deafening sound. I remember the isolation in the eyes of the men in the jail that day. It was the look of separation from those they loved. I remember the cold and uncomfortable feel of the steel and cement surroundings that we worshipped in that day. It was not a natural place of celebration. Yet, despite all that, there was God, right there in our midst. Behind the locked doors, among these troubled men, in these unpleasant surroundings, there was God! I knew that I would be coming back."

Gerry Quinlivan

CHAPTER THREE

Who Is An Inmate?

For all have sinned, and come short of the glory of God;
Romans 3:23

According to the American Correctional Association,
which supplied the statistics for this chapter, there were
2,033,331 inmates held in federal and state prisons or in
local jails at the end of 2002.

One of them is Steve, a former inmate of one of Ohio's most notorious prisons. Steve had reformed and was living a productive life with a good job and a long-term relationship. Steve had been living "trouble free" for five years, when a seven-year-old felony assault warrant from another state caught up with him. At the time of his arrest, Steve had connected with a local church and was earnestly seeking the Lord. Now he wonders how going back to prison could possibly be God's will for his life.

97,491 women were under the jurisdiction of state or
federal prison authorities.

One of them is April, doing a four year sentence in Alabama for drug offenses. April has connected with a correspondence ministry that has helped her change her life. She's praying for a transfer to a work-release program where she will be able to support herself and have more opportunity to see her son and daughter. She sometimes becomes depressed at her powerlessness to affect the lives of her children, but she has Christian friends to lean on now, and she understands the importance of staying connected with the body of Christ when she is released.

51% of inmates were under the influence of drugs or alcohol at the time of their current offense.

One of them is Danny. A casual drug user since his youth in the military, Danny became addicted to cocaine and crack in his early fifties. Drug use had never prevented Danny from holding a good job before, but crack addiction caused him to lose interest in everything but crack. Danny started committing petty crimes and forgeries to support his addiction, then turned to armed robbery. One day Danny robbed two banks and fled the state. He quickly went through the money buying drugs and alcohol. On the verge of suicide, Danny walked into a church in Mississippi and told his story to a pastor, who patiently listened, then courageously led this armed, desperate fugitive to Christ. Danny turned himself in and is now doing ten years in a maximum security prison. A new Christian, hungry for the Lord, Danny seeks spiritual guidance and support from other Christians in this hard and hostile environment.

9% of inmates were homeless in the 12 months prior to their arrest.

One of them is Tyrone, who built a small fire in an abandoned building for warmth on a freezing night. When the fire spread, Tyrone panicked and ran out of the building. Two of Tyrone's companions died in the blaze. Now, awaiting trial on two counts of manslaughter, Tyrone pores over a donated bible and wonders if God will punish him.

As Christians, we must see people where the world sees statistics. To do otherwise is to reduce inmates to something less than beings created in the image of God. Every inmate has a story and those stories are born of facts like the following information supplied by the U. S. Department of Justice:

* 31% of jail inmates had grown up with a parent or guardian who abused alcohol or drugs.

* 12% had lived in a foster home or institution.

* 46% had a family member who had been incarcerated.

* 50% of the women in jail said they had been physically or sexually abused in the past, compared to 10% of the men.

The statistics can be frightening: 3.1 %, or, 1 in every 32 American adults, is in jail, prison, or on parole. 46% of inmates were incarcerated for an offense of violence. 64% of prison inmates are of a racial or ethnic minority. Only 28% of jail inmates are there on their first offense.

The numbers can seem overwhelming, and there is an inclination to shrug your shoulders and ask, "What can one person do?"

Again, we must look through the numbers and see the people. We have a tendency to believe that if we can't do it all, we shouldn't try to do anything. You can't affect 2,033,331 inmates, but you can pray with Steve. You can't comfort 97,941 women, but you can write April an encouraging letter. You can't cure over a million inmates of alcoholism or drug addiction, but you can be a friend to Danny. You can't provide homes for Tyrone and thousands of other homeless Americans, but you can give them the opportunity to worship with Christian brothers and sisters who care about them.

This chapter opened with Romans 3:23. We must never enter a jail or prison with a spirit of superiority or righteousness. All have sinned, including those who minister. Violators of civil law are sinners, as described in Romans 13:1-5, but not all sins are violations of civil law. Adultery, for example, is a terrible sin, but in our society it is not punished by civil law. In 1 Corinthians 6, Paul mentions ten behaviors that prevent a person from inheriting the kingdom of God. Only two of those, theft and extortion, are civil crimes, and a third, drunkenness, is only a crime under certain conditions.

I have the honor of being acquainted with a very godly man in my church named Burt. Burt is a retired phone company employee, and he and his wonderful wife Ginny are truly salt and light to our community. When Burt learned that I had begun a jail ministry, he came to me and told me how he used to go into the jail to repair the telephones and he would look at the inmates and think "there but for the grace of God, go I." This seems like a strange statement from a man of God and solid citizen like Burt, but the fact is, Burt gets it. Burt understands that we all have a sin nature. Some sin lands us in jail and some sin doesn't.

Chapter Three

If we truly believe Romans 3:23, instead of entering the institution with a feeling of superiority, we should leave the institution with a prayer of thanksgiving.

Nothing that I have written in this chapter should be interpreted as an attempt to infer that most inmates should not be locked up. Many of them are dangerous. Some should never be permitted to re- enter society. Some will refuse to be rehabilitated. Some are so unrepentant that they continue to commit serious crimes while in prison.

All of them, however, were created by God, in the image of God, to have a relationship with God. Jesus Christ was crucified to redeem them all. As followers and disciples of Jesus Christ, we are commissioned to serve them by bringing them the gospel and giving them the opportunity to worship.

What is an inmate? We can build a statistical model of a "typical" inmate: male, African American, aged 27 years, high school educated, incarcerated on a drug charge, in his second term of imprisonment.

But "typical" thinking is worldly thinking. "Typical" thinking demonizes the inmate and allows us to dismiss him and go our way without giving him a second thought. "Typical" doesn't tell us that he has a grandmother who prays for him but is too infirm to make the three-hour trip to visit, that he worries that his younger brother will quit school and end up in prison, or that he longs for true Christian fellowship. The statistical model doesn't tell us the background story, doesn't let us see the fear and regret, doesn't let us experience the shame and hopelessness of being behind bars.

Every inmate is an individual, fearfully and wonderfully made by our creator. Every inmate has a story, and each of those stories has value. Crossroad Bible Institute, an international correspondence ministry that serves scores of thousands of inmates worldwide, calls prisoners, "the least, the lost and the last." There are 2.3 million of the least, the lost and the last in America, and all of them need something that you can give them.

The Hard Stare

Some of these trips are to a place that handles kids who are separated from their parents because at least one of the two parties wants it that way. The trouble these kids face is so foreign to me. They have prayer requests that include, "Thank you, God that I wasn't shot this week, "and" Pray for my cousin who was killed last night."

My heart aches when I read and pray over their prayer requests. One Sunday, as we were singing worship songs, there was a boy of about 15 looking at me with an angry stare. I often smile as I sing worship songs, and each time I returned his gaze, I found his hard stare unwavering. I prayed for direction from God as I sang, seeking guidance about whether to ignore the boy or look back. Then I turned to look back in his direction and I continued to sing with a smile on my lips as I sang.

After a while, he broke the stare, and his anger disappeared. It never returned during the rest of our time together. I read

Chapter Three

a devotional that described the Hebrew people in the wilderness complaining they were thirsty. Certainly water is essential to life. But it went on to say that what they needed more than water was assurance that they were not alone in the wilderness. Looking back, I think this boy was like that. What he needed more than anything was the assurance that despite his troubled situation, he was not alone. I believe God met him that morning and gave him that reassurance.

Gerry Quinlivan

How do you affect the lives of 2.3 million people? It seems like an impossible task, but we find inspiration in the ministry of Jesus. We know from scripture that Jesus addressed great crowds on several occasions, but very little is written about those events. What is described in detail, and powerfully so, is Jesus' ministry to individuals, one-on-one. The woman at the well, the demoniac in the Gaderene tombs, Nicodemus, the paralytic at Bethesda, and so many more, are example to us of the power of ministering one-on-one. In the next four chapters you will read about how that can be done by Christian laymen.

Here is one story of how one lay volunteer can change the life of an inmate, and through that single act, affect change in many.

Jessica and the Gospel of John

Jessica was an inmate at River City Correctional Facility. I would guess her to be about eighteen years old. We met near the end of the hour we get to spend with the prisoners. She came up to me and asked me if I would pray for her. I told

40

her that I would be honored to pray with her, and asked her if there was a specific need she wanted prayer for. It seemed like such an innocent, standard question. She looked at me for a moment as if to see if I was serious, then she really opened up. She told me that last year her mother had committed suicide on Mother's Day. When they got home from the cemetery, her stepfather told her that he couldn't take care of all the children, and since she was the oldest, she'd have to leave. She had nowhere to go, no job, no money, no relatives, no skills or even a high school diploma. She left home with only the clothes on her back and wound up living on the streets or with whoever would take her in. I don't know how she wound up in jail and it doesn't matter. She was worried; she had only four months left on her sentence and she had no idea what she would do or where she would go when she was released. I told her how much God loved her and how He would provide for her if she would just trust Him. She was receptive, so I explained the plan of salvation to her.

I asked her if she wanted to give her life to Christ and she said yes. I had a Pocket Testament League Gospel of John booklet in my pocket, I took it out and we read the prayer of commitment together. I found it very fulfilling to be able to give this blessed hope in such a desperate situation. I gave her the booklet and encouraged her to read the Gospel of John. A month later, I was checking the Pocket Testament League website and found that Jessica had ordered 11 pocket testaments. Jessica was now sharing the hope that I had given her. I get excited thinking about how God used me to touch people I've never met.

Ed Hoffman

CHAPTER FOUR

Praise And Worship Team Ministry

*But ye shall receive power, after that the Holy Ghost is
come upon you: and ye shall be witnesses unto me both in
Jerusalem, and in all Judea, and in Samaria, and unto
the uttermost part of the earth.*
Acts 1:8

The most common, and most important, form of jail and
prison ministry is praise and worship ministry. In this
ministry, we do in the institution what we do in our church
building on Sunday morning. This is a team ministry, and
team members should be from the same church. This ministry
gives the opportunity for you to reach large numbers of
inmates in a short time and give them the opportunity to
attend church services or bible studies. Since inmates can't
come to church, the church has to come to them.

At this point, I must stress that pastoral support and the
support of your church body is of utmost importance to this
ministry. When you go into the institution for praise and
worship, you take your whole church with you. Even if only
five or six are there in the flesh, the spirit of your whole
church will be there. Before exploring this ministry, make
absolutely sure that such support is available. Your ministry
will not bear fruit otherwise.

Praise And Worship Team Ministry

I have served in praise and worship ministries that were "tolerated" by the church, but not supported. Those ministries were stagnant, lifeless and ineffective. I never saw a soul won to Christ in those ministries. I now lead a team that gets regular encouragement from the pulpit, goes in to the jail with prayer cover, and is warmly supported by the church membership. The team goes into the institution with a sense of purpose, models Christian joy to the inmates, and sees conversions frequently.

One element of church support is knowing that you can tell an inmate that he will be welcome if he comes to your church. Inmates will often ask that, sometimes sincerely, and sometimes as a test of your sincerity.

In Matthew 9:12 -13, Jesus says "...They that be whole need not a physician, but they that are sick. But go ye and learn what that meaneth, I will have mercy, and not sacrifice: for I am not come to call the righteous, but sinners to repentance."

Church members should welcome all sinners to fellowship, and those who can't should take a look within themselves.

How One Member Got Started

I received a letter in the mail from my pastor encouraging me to consider joining a new jail ministry being started at our church. In fact, that personal invitation is what prompted me to check it out. I have some other ministry responsibilities on Sunday morning, so I would probably not have become involved without that extra encouragement. I'm glad that I did. I had never really thought about jail ministry before. I had never been a part of a church that had one, and it's not the

43

kind of thing I would jump into on my own. The upfront training made it easy to be involved, and the time commitment was simple as well. Team members return in time for our church's 11:00 worship service. Personally, I find that I come to church with a heart better prepared to worship when I have already been worshipping and serving in the jail earlier the same day.

Gerry Quinlivan

Many inmates will have their first exposure to the love of Jesus Christ through this ministry. An inmate who doesn't know the Lord will probably not seek out a chaplain or associate with Christian inmates. But he may, out of curiosity or boredom, and emboldened by being part of a group, attend a worship service. Some who do not appear to be attending will be listening from inside a cell or around a corner in a hallway. Man was created to be in communion with God, and inmates will be drawn to worship services even when they don't know why.

Jail and prison worship services are very important to the believers who are housed in the institution. A worship service reminds them that they are still in the family of God, still connected to Christians outside the prison walls, still loved and cherished by the creator of the universe.

Because of the opportunity to reach the unchurched and its importance to incarcerated believers, I believe that praise and worship ministry is the most important of the lay jail and prison ministries. It is this ministry that may inspire an inmate to contact a chaplain, to become involved in Christian correspondence, to attend an event or revival. This ministry also most closely models the New Testament church of the book of Acts, a church that was not a building, but a living, dynamic movement that went forth into homes, stables, shops, the streets and jails.

For this reason, the praise and worship ministry must be well planned and well organized. It must be your "first fruits". It must be as good a "product" as what you produce for your church's Sunday morning service.

So this ministry must not be entered into "lightly". You will be making a commitment to the institution, to the inmates, and to God to provide this service. You must make sure that you have the resources and manpower not just to start this ministry, but to sustain it.

Luke 14:28 reads, "For which of you, intending to build a tower, sitteth not down first, and counteth the cost, whether he have sufficient to finish it?"

It is a terrible witness to show up late, understaffed, or unprepared. It is worse to not show up at all; disregarding a commitment to the institution, the inmates and God.

If you do not feel confident that your church can sustain or support this type of ministry, pray about it. Talk it over with your pastor and elders. If the support is not there, or if the human resources are not available, explore one of the other forms of jail and prison ministry described in the following chapters. I don't suggest that you try to be a "one man show". It has been done, and it can be done, but it takes an extraordinarily dedicated and talented individual to do a complete worship service on his own.

Chapter Four

What makes a "complete" service? At the minimum, it should consist of music, a sermon or bible study, a time of corporate prayer, and a period of fellowship and individual prayer. You should do what you do in your church, as closely as you can model it in the correctional setting. If God has called *your* church into the jail and prison ministry, He wants you to be *your* church. Don't try to do what some other church does because that church seems to be successful in ministry. God already has *that* church; now He wants *yours*. Play the music your church plays, dress the way people dress in your church, and give the kind of message your church gives.

Keep the music simple. Use live music if you have musicians available and if the institution allows instruments. Guitars and portable keyboards are usually acceptable. If you have no available musicians, use a portable CD/tape player. Make sure that you use battery operated players and keyboards; a source of electricity will probably not be available. Expect all instruments and appliances to be thoroughly inspected by staff. Make sure your equipment is ready and batteries are fresh. Lack of preparation in this area can lead to embarrassment and disappointment:

The Wrong Song and a Broken String

I've found that it's a really good idea to prepare for what you're going to do and say in a worship service. I've also found that you need to be open to where the Lord leads you. During one service, I began to lead the first song. After about 20 seconds of solo, one of the team members told me that the song I was singing wasn't on the song sheet that had been passed out to the inmates. Oops...Oh well, that's OK, I thought, I try to memorize most of the music we use anyway, so I took one of the song sheets and began to play the first song. About halfway through that song one of my guitar strings broke. Oops again...we finished the rest of the music a capella with a little accompaniment of drumming on the back of the guitar. I can tell you that I don't want that to happen again, but I can also say that if God uses circumstances like that to reach His children, I still want to be part of it.

Kirk Hopkins

I have found that it's best not to try to anticipate what type of music the inmates may appreciate. Do what you do best; don't try to be someone else. Most inmates are so grateful for the opportunity to worship that they'll be happy with whatever you provide.

The style of dress is also a concern; again, be yourself as much as the institution regulations permit. As mentioned earlier in this book, there are three concerns about dress: modesty, safety and culture.

Modesty will usually be regulated by the institution and will apply to all visitors and staff. Sleeveless shirts and blouses, short trousers, short skirts, low necklines or any type of clothing which brings attention to the body (male or female) will generally not be permitted. Coats and jackets may not be permitted in the inmate areas. Open-toed shoes are not permitted.

The biggest safety concern is very simple: don't dress like the inmates. If there is trouble in the institution, staff must be able to distinguish visitors from inmates at a glance. Avoid wearing the same colors as inmate uniforms. This can vary from institution to institution, so do your homework and check it out beforehand. Ties and scarves may not be permitted in some high security areas since they could possibly used to choke the wearer. Expensive jewelry and watches should be left at home and purses should be locked in the vehicle. Cell phones, PDA's and other electronic devices will probably not be permitted.

The culture aspect of clothing is controversial and a matter for each individual team to decide. Some believe that you should dress formally and professionally to show your best out of respect for God. Others believe that since inmates are dressed very casually, formal dress on the part of the team accentuates the status of the inmate and creates a gulf between the inmates and the team. This is a philosophical issue and there is merit to both sides. If you have no strong feelings either way, fall back on the first principle--be yourself.

Preparation for your worship service is critical because of the environment. Most prisons and jails are chaotic, and inmates soon learn to take advantage of chaos. Rehearse your music and messages so you make the most of your available time. Unstructured "gaps" in the service will allow the inmates time to take control of the service. You will find a lot of "frustrated preachers" in jails and prisons, and if you let them get a "foot in the door", they will take over. If you are going to include inmate participation in your service, like testimonies or prayer requests, do that at the end of your service, after you have accomplished your music, message and prayer. Matthew 10:16 reads, "Behold, I send you forth as sheep in the midst of wolves: be ye therefore wise as serpents, and harmless as doves." Always be wary of an inmate who wants to speak during your service or sing a solo. If you allow the inmate to do that, have him do it at the end of your service, or you might find him monopolizing all your time. Your team has an hour or two once a week in the institution, that inmate is there 24/7, let him preach or sing on his time, not yours. Allowing inmates to "steal the show" will render you ineffective. Consider this story of failure:

Testimony Day

I was once part of a worship team that was chronically unprepared. One Sunday morning, the member who was supposed to give the message informed us that he was "led" to allow inmates to give testimonies instead. The inmates eagerly volunteered to take their place in the "pulpit". The first confessed to having had a fifty-dollar-a-day drug habit, being a five hundred-dollar-a-day drug dealer, and threatening customers who didn't pay up. The second confessed to having a hundred-dollar a day drug habit, being a thousand-dollar-a-day dealer, and beating up customers who didn't pay up. The third claimed a thousand-dollar-a-day habit, five-thousand per day in deals, and breaking the legs of slow payers. During this testimony snickering and open laughter could be heard from the inmates as each new speaker tried to "top" the one before him. By the time we got to the millionaires who had their clients murdered there were catcalls and horse laughs coming from the crowd. There was no way we could regain control, and we left the pod shamefaced and defeated. Not only had we not gained any ground for Jesus Christ, we had allowed the enemy to rout us, and it was because one member failed to do what he had committed to do--prepare and deliver a message.

Prayer and preparation are your best defenses against

something like this happening. Each team member should be in prayer prior to the day of the worship service, and the team should join for group prayer prior to entering the institution. A prayer warrior on the outside or back at your church praying for protection of the team while the service is being held is also a great help

The message you bring with your worship service should be a message of hope, salvation or healing. You will be addressing people from wide background of faith traditions, and doctrinal issues are not a good subject for the message. Some of your audience will have never been to a church before and will be unaware of denominational differences. Keep it simple, keep it hopeful, and lift up Jesus Christ.

Leave some time at the end of your service for fellowship and one-on-one prayer. Our team has seen many conversions because of this relationship building time. Be open to movements of the Holy Spirit during this fellowship.

Ask Him!

I met Markus during the summer of '04 at the Queensgate Correctional Facility. We started our visit with prayer and worship. I read a short devotional and then Jim gave the message. I found the message inspiring because Jim lifted up Jesus and explained His saving power. After the message we had corporate prayer and then broke up into small groups for fellowship. That's when I saw Markus. He was off by himself and looked like he felt out of place. I went over to him and started a conversation--just small talk; how are you getting along, etc. He would answer my questions, but seemed preoccupied and agitated. He started telling me that he thought he was basically a good person. I knew the Holy Spirit was working on him as he rethought Jim's message. I tried to continue with small talk, but the Holy Spirit was working on me, too! I kept hearing a voice in the back of my mind saying "Ask him!". I knew what I was supposed to ask, but I was afraid. What if he said no? What if he laughed at me? Finally it seemed that no matter what I tried to say, the only words that would come out of my mouth were "the question". So I threw caution to the wind and asked, "Would you like to give your life to Christ?" The reply was immediate--yes, he would. I was shocked! I had made it so difficult in my mind that his answer caught me off guard. I led him in the sinner's prayer, and our time was up and I had to leave.

I don't remember much about leaving the jail that day. I was so overwhelmed that God could use someone like me for such an important task. I know that Markus hadn't been impressed by my conversation. God had done the hard work, all I had to do was be there and be faithful by opening my mouth. I've never felt so alive as at that moment when God's hand was on me. It was an experience I hope to repeat over and over! Now, when we make our jail visits, I look for the signs of God working in the hope that He will use me again.

Ed Hoffman

After the service, have the team stay together for a short "debriefing" to share experiences and critique the service. My church allows us to use the church van for transportation to the jail, and we have some great conversations on the way back to church after the service. It's an excellent "team building" opportunity, and strong relationships are forged in the shared joy of ministry. We occasionally do services at a youth facility and we've had some very moving experiences there. We were all particularly inspired by this story, when a young man dropped his mask and gained his salvation.

Prayer of Salvation

I have the privelege of leading the music on our jail ministry team at the youth facility. As we were concluding one worship service, we sang a song about repentance. At the end of the song, I started praying aloud. In the middle of the prayer, I was strongly led to offer the young people the opportunity to join me in the prayer of salvation. I told them that if they wanted to pray with me, they could, or if they wanted to pray silently, that was OK, too.

Now here's the amazing part: One of the young men stood and prayed out loud with me! This just about blew me off my feet! I had not originally planned on praying, and I had never led a group in the prayer of salvation, and I would never have guessed that a young teenager in jail would have the courage to say that prayer out loud with about 30 of his peers sitting around him. God is good, all the time. I still pray for that young man today.

Kirk Hopkins

Reverend Jack Marsh, the Director of Justice Chaplaincies in the greater Cincinnati area, has composed this list of attributes for jail and prison worship teams. If you are considering this ministry, it's worthwhile to keep them in mind.

Be who you are.

Do what you do when your church meets for worship within the time and space limitations of the facility. Be yourselves as individuals and as a group.

Be honest.

When you are asked a question, answer it clearly, honestly and directly as you can. We do not agree on all things, but we can be honest and straightforward about what we believe.

Be respectful.

The purpose of this ministry is to give those incarcerated the opportunity to get in touch with the spiritual part of their lives and to find help and comfort in God. For many of us, our beliefs are very similar. On some things we believe differently. Your focus ought not to be on doctrine, disagreements or the problems with other faiths. Therefore...

Be focused on the positives.

Some themes that are appropriate are: Who is God? Is forgiveness possible? Can my life be any different? Does God really love me? How can I change? Use the themes of love, hope, forgiveness, peace and reconciliation.

Be prepared.

Know what you want to do and say. Never preach from your doubts and uncertainties. If you aren't clear about something, you can't expect others to be. Services "planned" after you get in the door are at best risky and, at worst, confusing and a hindrance to faith.

Be pleasant.

Chapter Four

You go there to worship with the inmates, but you make a witness to all with whom you come into contact. Many officers have said how much they like certain teams; some even attend the services themselves. A smile, a greeting, and a kind word go a long way. You have many opportunities to minister in the jail. Don't be doom and gloom in your attitude--there's enough of that in the jail already.

Be obedient.
Follow all requests or directions of corrections officers. After all, they are in charge, we are visitors.

If you are interested in starting a worship team ministry, contact your local jail or prison for details and a contact person. If your local institution has no worship ministry, make an appointment with the administrator and discuss the possibility of starting one.

CHAPTER FIVE

Lay Chaplaincy

...but woe to him that is alone when he falleth;
he hath not another to help him up.
Ecclesiastes 4:10

If being part of a jail or prison worship team is not a possibility for you, or if you want to spend more time with inmates than worship ministry allows, you may want to explore lay chaplaincy. Lay chaplains generally serve under the leadership of a professional or ordained chaplain, and volunteer their time giving spiritual counsel and comfort to inmates. Lay chaplains may also distribute bibles and other religious literature and conduct bible studies or small group ministries within the jail or prison.

Unlike "pastor", "bishop", "elder", "preacher", "teacher", "deacon" or "evangelist", "chaplain" is not a scriptural term, and its exact meaning is elusive. Generally described as "a religious presence in a secular institution", the duties or job description of a chaplain may vary widely from institution to institution. In some institutions lay chaplains operate independently. In others they operate in pairs or teams in the presence of the ordained chaplain. Some institutions are very rigid in determining the exact mission of the lay chaplains. Others are less restrictive, allowing lay chaplains to seek out their own ministries within the institution.

Chapter Five

For example, in the jail system where I serve as a lay chaplain, one of the volunteers has built a ministry around the distribution of reading glasses. Many inmates rarely read on the outside, and when they are incarcerated they find that their eyesight has diminished. Since this problem is not really a medical necessity, the institution does not provide reading glasses.

This volunteer obtains glasses from flea markets, discount stores and private donations (as well as his own funds), and distributes them to inmates who submit a request form (kite). This is an opportunity to connect with the inmate, offer prayer and possibly establish a relationship for the purpose of spiritual guidance.

Another volunteer, who is a very gifted bible teacher, has been given permission to conduct bible studies one night per week in the chapel. These are so popular with the inmates that attendance is always "standing room only", and the number of attendees has to be regulated by the administration.

These are just two of many "niche" ministries that volunteers have been able to fill within the jail system.

The primary mission of the lay chaplain, however, is to be a friend to the inmate. Not a friend in the sense that many inmates may define friendship, but a friend in the biblical sense, as in the verse that opened this chapter. You must be a friend as in Proverbs 27:17, "Iron sharpeneth iron; so a man sharpeneth the countenance of his friend". We must be the kind of friend that comes alongside and offers true support, not just kind words for itching ears.

It may be very difficult to think of yourself befriending someone in a jail or prison. After all, some of these people have done unspeakable things. What common ground could you possibly have with a prostitute or armed robber?

Jesus was called a "friend of sinners" by the Pharisees, and He didn't deny it. Like Jesus, we must meet people where they are, establish healthy relationships, and give them the good news of the love of Jesus Christ.

The people who populate corrections facilities are no better or worse than the people Jesus associated with in His ministry. Many of these men and women have never had a healthy relationship. They've never had a true friend or confidant. As a lay chaplain, you have the opportunity to model the love of Jesus Christ to them, to show them that a better way of life exists and to give them hope for the future.

Sometimes this involves "tough love" since many inmates you encounter are self-centered, in denial, or take a "victim's stance" about their present condition. We must model honesty to them, but we must do it in a loving way. Many inmates are victims of horrible abuse, and many are victims of permissiveness; they've never had anyone love them enough to tell them "no", to firmly guide them in the right direction, to teach them to control their passions and appetites. Through spiritual counseling, based on a biblical foundation, we can help an inmate turn his life in a new direction and be the person God created him to be.

It doesn't always work. Many are not open to the gospel and have no desire to live any way but the way they have been living. For those who do want a better way, we have the

Chapter Five

opportunity to be salt and light and to see the miracle of the Holy Spirit taking over someone's life:

Killer's Pod

One Sunday our worship team was assigned to the highest security area of the jail, a unit nicknamed "killer's pod" because almost everyone there was awaiting trial or sentencing for murder. It was an eventful service. During the praise and worship phase, officers raided a nearby cell and stopped an attempted rape. There was an inmate at the service who was disruptive, not disrespectful, but very hyperactive and noisy.

Despite these distractions it was a great service, and we felt the presence of the Holy Spirit working powerfully in the men. During the fellowship time a young man came up to me and told me that my message had moved him powerfully and he wanted to accept the invitation to bring Jesus into his heart. I had the privilege of leading him in the "sinner's prayer" and telling him about the next steps. Later that week I visited him and began to disciple him.

A week or two later I received a letter at church from another inmate in that unit. He had been referred to me by the young man that I was discipling. The writer indicated that he knew about my law-enforcement background (I don't keep that a secret; whenever I'm asked about myself by an inmate, I answer honestly). Because of that, he specifically wanted to see me, not another chaplain. Since this was an odd request, I notified the officers in the unit about it before my visit.

When they called the inmate out to meet me, I was surprised to see that it was the man who had been so disruptive during the service. In the letter he had referred to some "unfinished business" between him and the Lord. I assumed that he wanted to accept Christ as the other man had, but that wasn't it. He told me that he wanted to tell me "his story" so that there would be someone who could understand and pass it on to others to prevent them from becoming like him.

He was agitated and hyper, but not as bad as he had been that Sunday. I listened for over three hours as he told me the story of his life, his estranged wife and children, and his tumultuous relationships with women and men, particularly with his co-defendant, a man he had met in a previous prison term. His tale was disjointed and repetitive, but it was also having a calming effect, as if he had been waiting a long time to get rid of it.

The major theme of his story was simple—at every crisis, at every trial, at every conflict, he turned away from God instead of toward God. He chose darkness over the light at every opportunity, and each step toward the darkness made its pull even stronger. He told me about his suicidal impulses, how he had bought a handgun to shoot himself, and the comforting feeling of walking around with the means of his own demise in his pocket.

He started to tell me about the crime that put him in the killer's pod, and I fought a strong impulse to pull a pad and pencil out of my briefcase and start taking notes--old habits die hard. It was an all too familiar story: an evening of drinking and drug use blending into a night of cruising, a stop at a gas station, and an impulsive, stupid decision to rob it.

Chapter Five

He looked at the clerk-- a father and husband moonlighting a second job to make ends meet--over the barrel of the handgun, and for no reason that he can articulate, squeezed the trigger, ending the life of a man who meant him no harm. He wept and I comforted him.

After a time of silence he told me why he wanted me to see him. "The police don't have the gun," he said. "I want you to give it to them".

I told him that if what he was about to tell me was a matter of public safety, my oath of confidentiality was void. I would have to give the police the information and tell them who it came from.

He told me that he didn't want confidentiality. I cautioned him again. He told me the reason he wanted to tell me was that he knew the police would believe me because I'm an ex-cop. He didn't want to tell them himself, and if he told anyone else in the jail, they'd use the information to bargain a lighter sentence for themselves.

He quickly told me where the gun was, drew a map of the apartment and pinpointed the exact location. When I asked him who the arresting officer was, I was surprised to learn that it was a sheriff's case, and I knew the detective well.

A search warrant was served and the murder weapon was found in the exact location he'd given. The detective was incredulous.

"The guy just gave himself life," the detective told me. "The case wasn't very strong and he was scheduled to go before the most lenient judge in the county. He might have walked without the evidence of the gun. He just convicted himsclf."

Actually, I believe he was convicted by the Holy Spirit.

I continued to meet with him while he awaited trial. He grew more and more at peace. We studied the bible together and eventually he gave his life to Jesus. We began to talk about personal evangelism and I got him some books on the subject. He wrote a letter of apology to his victim's widow. He pled guilty and got a life sentence. We write to each other often, and he takes bible correspondence courses. He wants to evangelize other inmates in prison. He told me it's the only way all this can make any sense.

The qualifications to be a lay chaplain will vary from institution to institution. A background check will be done and probably a drug test. A criminal background will not necessarily disqualify you. Some very good lay chaplains were saved in prison. But you will have to be conviction-free for a minimum of one year. Some prisons may not permit you to minister if you have former co-defendants or known associates within the prison. Most facilities will require at least a high-school diploma and a letter of recommendation from your pastor.

Training usually consists of legal issues for chaplains, confidentiality issues, prison regulations and the role of the chaplain in the institution. Most training programs also cover listening skills, relationship building, addiction recognition and available educational and post-release resources.

Chapter Five

You will probably not be trained in theology, discipleship or evangelism. You are expected to bring those skills with you. Being a good listener is the most valuable skill you can have in this ministry. Since most of the inmates have never had a healthy relationship, they have never had someone really listen to them and value what they have to say. Listening builds a relationship quickly and opens the door to the gospel. Everybody has a story, and if you take the time and effort to listen, every story is interesting. Once you know their story, they will probably ask for your story, which leads you to His story.

One of the duties you may take on as a lay chaplain is to notify an inmate of the illness or death of a loved one. Prison is not about confinement; prison is about powerlessness. Confinement is the means of powerlessness. While the inmate is incarcerated, life and death go on without him, and the news of personal tragedy hits them hard. The inmate may not even be permitted to attend the funeral. You are the friend he has to lean on at that time. Grief can bring on a spiritual awakening in a person, and you have the opportunity to not only offer comfort, but also salvation.

Unless you are in a high security facility that requires you to be in pairs, chaplaincy is generally a solitary ministry. In fact, the "confidant" aspect of chaplaincy almost demands that it is done in solitude.

I had some trouble getting used to that for two reasons. First, the biblical model is to be sent in pairs. Second, I have heard my pastor say, "If you are doing ministry by yourself, you're probably doing it wrong."

Lay Chaplaincy

For this reason, you should be spiritually rooted in a home church where you can get spiritual guidance and have an accountability partner or group where you can learn the type of biblical friend that you are to the inmates.

A good friend once told me that everyone should have a Timothy in their life, and everyone should have a Paul in their life. I think that's good advice.

Most of the time a lay chaplain will connect with a prisoner through a "kite"—an inmate's request to see a chaplain or get a bible or religious literature. Some institutions forbid "proselytizing" and you can only see an inmate in response to the inmate's request or a legitimate third party request.

I try to take advantage of every opportunity to establish a relationship. An inmate may simply want a bible because it's the only free thing available to read. I'll still try to get a conversation started. If that fails, I always ask the inmate if I can pray with him. It's very rare that someone refuses prayer. Even non-believers seem to sense that there is some kind of power in prayer. I have seen guys that were playing hard and shrugging off my attempts at conversation literally collapse in tears over being prayed with.

Prayer is a powerful bridge between people, and I use it at every opportunity. Once that contact is established, I ask the inmate if he'd like me to visit him again. Sometimes I'll say something like, "I think I can find some books that will help you understand that bible a little better. Would you like me to bring you one next week?"

Chapter Five

No inmate ever turns down anything that's free. When he says yes, I take that as an open invitation to visit any time, and I am not proselytizing.

One caution here: don't make a promise to an inmate unless you know you can keep it. If you say you will be back next Thursday at noon, that inmate will be counting on you to be there next Thursday at noon. There is very little to break the routine in jail or prison, and he will be anticipating your visit. To not show up is a poor witness.

It's actually best to be intentionally vague. "The next time I'm on this floor" or "when I can get back here again" are good phrases to use instead of an exact day and time.

Many inmates do not have to be coaxed into a relationship, and will be very natural and forthright with you. Sometimes their honesty is disarming.

Not Enough

An inmate in my area of the Justice Center put in a kite for a bible, and when I got to his pod and gave him the bible, I asked him if he wanted to talk for while. He said he was hoping he could talk to someone because he was depressed.

We sat down in the visiting area and I asked him to tell me about it. He said he'd only been in jail about a week, and it was quite some time since he'd been locked up. He had accepted Christ the last time he was in jail and he was trying to lead a better life. He'd connected with a church and was attending regularly. He was really disappointed that he'd been arrested again and felt like he'd let his church down.

He'd been drug-free for almost six months and was seeking employment. He had felt like quitting drugs would be the key to a better life, and he had actually been filling out a job application when the police raided his apartment and filed the charges that had him back in jail.

"I know now that just quitting drugs isn't enough to get me a better life," he said.

I was thrilled, thinking that he had a revelation that a relationship with Jesus was the key to life. I was eagerly anticipating hearing him say that when he continued, "Nope giving them up isn't enough...I've got to quit selling them, too!"

One last thing about lay chaplaincy: God loves them all and each of them is important to him. Bringing murderers and gang leaders to the Lord can be exhilarating, but remember that He wants the vagrants and "public nuisances", too. Don't "cherry pick" the notorious offenders out of some sense of prideful accomplishment. Just serve the Lord humbly and treat every inmate as someone of value.

Contact your local jail or prison for chaplaincy opportunities. Many juvenile facilities also use lay volunteers, as do drug and alcohol rehab facilities.

CHAPTER SIX

Event Ministries

Turn us again, O LORD God of hosts,
cause thy face to shine; and we shall be saved.
Psalm 80:19

Worship team ministries serve a moderate number of inmates on a regular, consistent basis; event ministries serve large numbers of inmates on a sporadic basis. Volunteers whose work or family responsibilities prevent them from making a commitment to worship team or lay chaplaincy ministries may find an opportunity to serve in event ministries.

Event ministries rarely occur more than twice a year in any given institution. These events last from one-half day to three days, require a great number of volunteers and are often sponsored by several churches working cooperatively.

Event ministries range from highly structured international organizations like Kairos, Residents Encounter Christ (REC), and Bill Glass Day of Champions, to local church revivals or crusades.

When the Billy Graham Crusade comes into an area the organizers usually attempt to create some kind of event in local jails and prisons. The formats of these ministries are highly diverse, from seminar style to tent revival.

The primary goal of event ministries is evangelism or revival. Some, like the Kairos program, attempt to build the Christian community in the institution by equipping Christian leaders among the inmates.

Some of the more organized event ministries will start preparing months before the event with weekly meetings for team-building activities, prayer and rehearsal of talks, testimonies and music. Very strong friendships can develop in this process, along with a great sense of teamwork and purpose.

Local churches benefit greatly by having members exposed to this leadership training. Teams will generally consist of a combination of ordained and lay volunteers. Most of the team will have inmate contact, but some members will be in a support role.

Because events can take on the elements of a show or performance, team members must work on maintaining a servant's heart and an attitude of humility. Teams need speakers, discussion leaders, musicians, singers, technicians and drivers.

Since event ministries use larger numbers of volunteers than worship ministries, and the volunteers are not "regulars", event ministries create a substantial security risk for the institution. Training in the rules and regulations of the facility should be a part of team training. Teams must be formed and train several weeks before the event so that background checks and drug screens can be cleared.

Chapter Six

Some states will require TB tests or other medical processes for the volunteers.

The methods of event ministries will vary based on length of the event and specific goals. They can include musical performances, preaching, testimony, speeches, small group discussions, prayer, fellowship, special appearances by noted athletes or entertainers and even special food "treats" for the inmates. Some events will also offer baptisms.

Events are very dynamic and can be highly emotional. Altar calls will result in a high percentage of inmates "coming forward". I worked an event ministry at a small state prison in Indiana where 50% of the attendees gave or re-dedicated their lives to Christ. You will see remarkable movements of the Holy Spirit during these events, and lives will truly change. Eyes and hearts will be opened to the Love of Jesus during events

The Motherless Child

I learned two things when I was asked to lead worship for an REC weekend: I learned how God could use me as a worship leader despite my initial fears, and I learned the way the Holy Spirit uses worship music to touch hearts.

When we began putting the music together for the weekend we had no idea who the group of residents were or how they would respond. We tried to use music that would reach the broadest group possible, so we opted to blend in rock-music-based worship songs with traditional southern-style hymns. I see now that this decision was driven by the Lord.

Jesus used our willingness and our prayer to be his "instruments"-no pun intended.

What began as a weekend of two timid groups—the worship team and the residents—coming together unsure of one another, became a single group of men unafraid to sing our praises to Jesus and to give God the glory for his movement among us during our time together. As we held hands in a long line and sang "Sanctuary" and "I Exalt Thee" with tears in our eyes, the Spirit filled every inch of that dingy yellow gym, and even the hardest of the hard men in the room could not escape it.

One moment I will never forget is when Virgil, the inmate all the others bragged on as their candidate for "Star Search" took the stage with us. Virgil sat in a chair in the middle of our makeshift stage with only an acoustic guitar and a microphone. As he began to sing "Sometimes I feel like a motherless child... a long, long way from home..." the room was stilled by the emotion in his words and the power in his voice. As soon as he finished the song, he collapsed, sobbing, into a pool of tears. The next thing I knew, Virgil was surrounded by both inmates and the REC team and he was being lifted up in prayer to comfort him. For a brief moment, I could feel the arms of Jesus around all the "motherless children" in the room, comforting them all with His grace and love. I had been told before I made the decision to be on the team that we would bless the inmates and, in doing so, be blessed ourselves. In hindsight, that seems like an understatement. I have never before, or since, felt such rich blessings from the Lord as I did during that weekend.

Russell Griffith

Chapter Six

There is a tremendous sense of accomplishment in participating in a successful event. I believe that it is similar to what is described in Luke 10:17, " And the seventy returned again with joy, saying, Lord, even the devils are subject unto us through thy name."

The Card

At the closing of the three-day event, inmates were invited to the podium to share their experiences with the group. Several took advantage of the opportunity, and there were some very moving testimonies.

I was surprised to see a young man named Terry approach the stage. Terry was a shy, nervous young man who had been profoundly moved during the event. He was certainly not the type of guy who enjoyed public speaking.

As he stood behind the podium, he pulled a worn greeting card from his pocket. It was obvious that the card was something he always carried with him. As tears coursed down his cheeks he told us that his mother had committed suicide just after he had been sent to prison, and a couple of days after he had been informed of her death he had received that card. His mother had written "You will always be loved, you will never be alone" on the card and then signed it. It may have been the last thing she had ever done.

Sobbing openly, Terry told us that until this event, he had never understood what those words meant, but after three days of seeing, hearing and feeling the love of Jesus Christ, he now knew that, indeed, he would always be loved, and he would never be alone.

One word of caution: beware of events that provide no "follow up" or relationship maintenance opportunities. It is irresponsible to evangelize large numbers of inmates and leave them without discipling resources. Among professional chaplains, this practice is known as "bible bombing."

Kairos and Residents Encounter Christ, among other event ministries, establish "communities" in the institution and arrange for regularly scheduled reunions for inmates and volunteers. Ministry should always involve relationships and event ministries that do not provide opportunities for relationship building are not mirroring the ministry of Jesus Christ.

In the third chapter of Mark, after preaching to a multitude, Jesus was told that his mother and brothers were seeking him. Verse 34 of that chapter reads, "And he looked round about on them which sat about him, and said, 'Behold my mother and my brethren!'"

These comments came from inmates attending a Residents Encounter Christ Program at a prison in southern Indiana:

"Before I came to the REC, I considered myself a religious person, but now I know I never really had a relationship with Jesus. I feel more love than ever before, especially in prison, where everything's negative. It's just good to have something positive."

Adam, Cambridge City

Chapter Six

"It (the REC weekend) really deepened my faith. It's catapulted me to a whole new level. It's so overwhelming, experiencing a deeper depth of God's love."

Theo, Indianapolis

"I was a Christian before attending the event, but now I feel equipped to teach my children about God when I'm released. We need more programs like this for offenders so we can share the same atmosphere and love with the rest of the world. I just wish it could keep going."

William, Ft. Wayne

Each of the event ministries mentioned here has a website with specific information including local contacts and schedules of events. Other web resources for event ministries are The Coalition of Prison Evangelists (COPE) and the website of the International Network of Prison Ministries, http://prisonministry.net

CHAPTER SEVEN

Correspondence Ministries

To the weak became I as weak, that I might gain the weak:
I am made all things to all men, that I might
by all means save some.
I Corinthians 10:22

Paul was ready to use all means to save men, and today's believers must be ready to use all means to minister and share the gospel. One of these means is correspondence, a powerful medium of communication which is becoming a lost art in the age of technology.

I first became aware of the power of the correspondence ministry when some men I had visited in the county jail asked me to write them when they were sent to prison. I had no idea how much mail meant to inmates and how much influence it could have on them. Many inmates receive regular visits from friends and family members while in their local jails awaiting trial. Once they are convicted and sent to a prison, sometimes more than a hundred miles from their home, the visits become more infrequent or stop altogether. Some inmates have burned all their bridges behind them and have nobody who will visit.

Mail is the only contact most inmates have with the outside world and, if nobody writes, the inmate feels cut off, forgotten. One inmate told me that his "cellie" fills out the subscription cards he finds in old magazines, just so he will occasionally get a form-letter bill for the publication. It's not much, but it breaks the routine.

The correspondence ministry is ideal for the person who cannot physically enter the institutions or is located in a geographical area where there is no access to jails or prisons. The major qualification is willingness. You do not have to be a skillful writer, a biblical scholar or a professional counselor. All you have to do is care. A simple greeting card with a few hand-written comments is sufficient to demonstrate the love of Jesus to someone starved for caring communications. Your correspondence can be a part of a bigger picture of Christ working in an inmate's life.

Consider this note written across the bottom of a correspondence bible lesson sent to an inmate at a state prison in Dayton, Ohio:

I just wanted to thank you for sending this course. I really enjoyed it. I also want to let you know that I am new to all this because I just turned my life over to the Lord on November 16, thanks to a jail ministry team in the Miami County Jail. I think what you guys are doing is great! God bless you all, and thanks again!

Mark, Dayton, Ohio

As Paul wrote in I Corinthians 3:6, "I have planted, Apollos watered; but God gave the increase." Your correspondence can be a part of that process.

74

When initially writing an inmate, always inquire about his relationship with Jesus Christ. I felt led to explain the plan of salvation to an inmate in Alabama several years ago and was blessed to get this letter in return:

Dear Brother Larry:

I would like to thank you for responding back to me. With your help, I have accepted Jesus Christ into my heart. And you were right—by accepting Jesus, my life has changed. Thank you for your prayers. I know that I will now have a second chance at life when I get out of here...

LaMarvin, Bessemer, Alabama

One major caution about correspondence ministry: there is no uniform set of rules for inmate correspondence. Each state and county has its own set of rules for what an inmate may receive in the mail. There may be a limit on number of pages. Books and magazines may have to be sent directly from a publisher. Some institutions allow you to send stamps, some allow only post office "embossed" envelopes, some allow neither. You may find mail regulations posted on the institution's website, or you may have to write the institution for them.

When I write the first letter to an inmate I ask him to send me the institution's mail regulations sheet in the next letter. If you do not follow the rules your letter will be confiscated and administrative action may be taken against the inmate.

Some inmates' mail may be regularly opened and inspected. This applies to incoming and outgoing mail. This should not matter but it is best to remain aware of possible censorship. Sending a letter deemed inappropriate by the administration may result in your being banned from corresponding with any inmate in that institution.

Since most correspondence ministers don't actually enter the facility, some inmates assume that the volunteer is unfamiliar with the rules of the institution and may request the volunteer to send contraband items. Beware of any "unusual" requests, especially for money or photographs.

There are three major forms of correspondence ministries: "Pen Pal" ministries, instructional (bible study) ministries, and a combination of the two. Before exploring these types of ministries there are some general correspondence guidelines to consider. The following guidelines are used by a combination instructional and pen pal ministry:

Believers Behind Bars Correspondence School of the Bible Inmate Correspondence Tips

1. Do not use your last name when writing to an inmate. The best way to avoid identity theft is to not fully identify yourself. You may trust the inmate with whom you are corresponding, but you don't know that another inmate won't have access to your letters.

2. Always use the Believers Behind Bars PO box as your return address. Do not divulge your home address or specific location.

3. Never send money, money orders, or checks. We provide spiritual support not financial.

4. Pray for guidance before writing.

5. Use scripture sparingly and when appropriate. In a ministry where I used to work, someone sent an inmate eight pages of handwritten bible verses. His response? "Hey, I already have a bible."

6. Be encouraging! Keep your letters light and upbeat until a relationship develops, then grow more serious if necessary.

7. Keep your first few letters short. After a couple of exchanges you will know more about the inmate and have more about which to write.

8. Don't ask the inmate why he is in prison. He may reveal that to you as trust develops. It should not matter to us anyway. Don't comment on, or correct, an inmate's grammar or spelling.

9. Be sensitive to the inmate's situation. Don't write detailed descriptions of vacations, family holidays, etc. Do be aware that holidays are very hard times in prisons. A special card or letter will always be welcome.

10. If the inmate has listed prayer requests in a previous letter, mention them in your next letter, so the inmate knows that you are praying for him and genuinely care about his concerns.

Chapter Seven

The Pen Pal ministry is the simplest form of correspondence ministry. There are several large agencies that administer this type of ministry, pairing inmates with correspondents and handling all administrative details. Some of these agencies are listed at the end of this chapter. These ministry agencies shield the volunteer's identity and provide a great deal of security.

Meeting inmates in other forms of jail and prison ministry can also be a source of contact for correspondence. Simply asking friends and church members if they know someone in prison may yield a contact. Even if you know the inmate personally, it is not a good idea to use your own address. Ask your pastor if you may use the church address, or get a post office box. PO Box prices vary according to location but can be rented for as low as $2.00 per month.

Many volunteers write to as many as a dozen inmates. The average turn-around on a letter is about two weeks, so if you budget a half-hour to an hour a day to write, you can easily take on several inmates if you want.

I believe that you should not write to an inmate of the opposite gender. Many male inmates want only a female to write to them. Some of the large pen pal ministries will pair volunteers with inmates of the opposite gender because of the sad reality that there are a lot more male inmates than female and a lot more females than males volunteer to write letters.

The pen pal ministry is very relational and often yields insight into the life of a prisoner:

Correspondence Ministries

...Prison life is a very controlled environment with exact times for every activity. There is plenty of time in the cell, an 8' x 12' room, which is kind of like living in a bathroom, minus the bath/shower and with a double bunk bed instead. It can be a lonely place at times, and I would enjoy writing to someone in order that we may cultivate a friendship that has true meaning; someone to fellowship with and share experiences, ideas, thoughts and inspirations. Your experiences in the real world would give me a touch of freedom in here...

Brad, Indian Springs, Nevada

The pen pal ministry is a very good choice for the outgoing, chatty personality. Your own "faith story" or witness may be a very good subject for an opening letter, but always remember that ministry is not about you. Inquire about the inmate's life and history and mention it frequently. Many inmates have a very low sense of self -value and believe that no one could be interested in them for themselves. This is an excellent opportunity to model the love of Jesus, who knows when each sparrow falls and values the inmate much more than any sparrow. As relationships grow, inmates will start to look beyond their own troubles and start to find a way to minister to others:

...Holidays are always hard in here, but we had a real nice Easter Sunday service, and I was able to go to chapel on Good Friday also. I really had a good time making up Easter baskets for the kids that came to visit their dads. It must be really hard for little kids to understand why they have to come here to see their fathers...

Danny, Lebanon, Ohio

Chapter Seven

The less extroverted volunteer may find himself better suited to the instructional correspondence ministry. There are several nationwide bible study ministries that use volunteers, some of which are listed at the end of this chapter. An individual or several church members can also start one of these ministries using Sunday school lessons or modular bible studies such as home-schooling materials. Make sure that you have permission to use the materials or that you use non-copyrighted studies.

The procedure for this ministry is simple: a lesson is mailed to the inmate, who completes the work and sends it back. The volunteer checks the work, grades it, writes some encouraging notes and sends it back to the inmate with the next lesson.

As mentioned in chapter one, recidivism is reduced by 61% in inmates who are involved in regular bible study programs. A diligent, continued study of God's powerful word will often help inmates get insight into their lives and the damage they have done. This awareness is instrumental in their healing.

My wife, Teri, received this letter from a woman who had a "victim" attitude when she started taking the study. Teri had encouraged her to "journal" her thoughts when studying:

...Two days after I finished your study on Deborah, I received a devotional called "Brave Heart, Deborah's Shout of Victory". It's amazing how things have come into accord since I started studying the bible. I find it happening again and again that something I study about comes into accord with what I'm doing in my life. I'm writing in my study journal daily, and there are so many tears as I feel the pain and hurt I have brought to my son and children and even my

grandchildren. In writing, I realized I needed to write my mom and dad, and I'm still working on that letter. So, writing and journaling is helping to cleanse me and helping me relate to my feelings and hurts. It also helps me give thanks for my blessings. Teri, you have been such a blessing to me. I go to God in thanksgiving and realize all He has given me by His grace and love...

Susette, Ypsilanti, Michigan

The word of God is sharper than a two-edged sword, and when an inmate immerses himself in the study of God's word, guided by a caring volunteer, his life can take on a new focus:

You know, my brother, spiritual growth takes time just like physical growth, so my main concern daily is living a life obedient to God's word. Sometimes I fall short, but when I do, I immediately ask God for forgiveness, then I keep pressing on. I find that many times when encouraging others that I also lift up my spirit. So I say to myself, what better place to test my Christianity. So continue to pray asking God to strengthen my ministry in reaching out to my fellow prisoners, because it's not about me; it's about Jesus.

Parris, Dayton, Ohio

Reviewing or grading the inmate student's lessons is a terrific opportunity to make constructive and encouraging comments that will have a very positive effect. Negative comments are seldom helpful. Many inmates are self-conscious of their poor reading and communications skills, but in response to positive suggestions, will apply themselves to the best of their ability. I have even had inmates tell me that they have applied for GED classes in order to be able to better study scripture. I don't believe that anything other than God's word would have that motivational power.

I received the lesson, and like always, it's good to hear from you. You mentioned in your comments that you admire my attitude and courage in facing this trial. I'd like you to know that along with constant praying, it's receiving encouraging notes from you and my family that keeps me going. I thank you for your love and concern; also I thank the prayer warriors at your church for their prayers and this ministry.

Parris, Dayton, Ohio

A combination Pen Pal and instructional ministry gives the inmates the benefits of both types, with the possible addition of getting input from more than one volunteer. In the Believers Behind Bars Correspondence School of the Bible, a ministry of my home church, I do all the administrative tasks, checking the incoming lesson, making encouraging comments, adding the new lesson and addressing the envelopes. I then turn the "packet" over to a volunteer assigned to that inmate and the volunteer writes a personal letter to the inmate. The inmate corresponds with the volunteer by placing a personal letter in the return envelope with the next study. In this system, the inmate maintains an instructor-student relationship with me, and a friend-mentor relationship with the volunteer. This is a double blessing for the inmate, who gets two relationships, a bible lesson, and a personal letter from a caring volunteer.

There are dozens of Christian pen pal ministries in need of volunteers. I highly recommend:

Christian Pen Pals PO
Box 2112 Staesville,
NC, 28687
There are many more listed at www.prisonministries.net, under the "pen pals" category.

The largest volunteer-run inmate correspondence bible course in the world is:
Crossroad Bible Institute of Grand Rapids Michigan, www.crossroadbible.org, or call 800-668-2450.

Many others can be found at www.prisonministries.net, under the category "bible schools."

If you are thinking of starting your own correspondence ministry, I advise working in one of the established ones for several months to "learn the ropes". Prior to starting Believers Behind Bars, I volunteered in Crossroads Bible Institute and Red Letter Ministries, an excellent regional ministry in Alabama.

When I felt led to start the Believers Behind Bars ministry, I wrote to several inmates and asked them to poll other inmates about what they liked and disliked about correspondence bible studies. Two comments kept showing up in the returns: "too short" and "too easy". I decided to fill a niche in correspondence ministry by providing challenging material in courses of long duration. Believers Behind Bars' longest course is 82 lessons. With an average turn around time of three weeks, it takes a student over four years to complete that course.

One of our students found our material a little too challenging, so he formed a four-man study group, and all four, working together nightly, complete the lesson. The formation of a bible study and fellowship small group was an unintended benefit of the ministry. Sometimes you just have to get out of the way and let God work.

AFTERWORD

Is It Really Worth the Trip?

*If the Son therefore shall make you
free, ye shall be free indeed.*
John 8:36

It's all about context. As I watched Max step up to the podium to address a group of men and women about his jail ministry efforts, I thought about context. Max had to tell us about his life as a prisoner before he could tell us about going into prison ministry. A real "there but for the grace of God go I" story, Max was a middle class, hard working, blue collar guy who developed a drinking problem. Max had some minor skirmishes with the law, typical for a drinker; then, a catastrophic fatal vehicle accident got Max an eight- year prison term, with a four-year minimum. Leaving a wife and child behind, Max went to prison.

Like so many others, Max knew Jesus as a youth, but turned his back on Him as a teenager. Fortunately for Max, Jesus never turned His back on Max:

"...and I cried out in my prison cell, 'Lord, I'm listening! What do you need? Change me! I've made a mess of my first 43 years, and whatever I have left, whether it's a day, or a week, or another 43 years, I'll give them to you

one day at a time.' And then I learned that God
doesn't call the cleaned, he cleans the called." -

- Max Huffman

Max had been a heavy smoker, and smoking was prohibited
in his institution. Tobacco was, however, available, and Max
knew that if he was caught smoking, he could have another
six months added to his sentence.

"I got down on my knees and begged God for deliverance
from my smoking habit, and immediately He brought into my
mind ten people who had witnessed to me through the years
their deliverance from tobacco addiction through divine
deliverance by the power of Jesus. The next day, when some
cigarettes were brought on the block, they called, 'Hey Max,
you in on this?' My desire for tobacco immediately
disappeared. I hollered 'No, I'm OK', and 'floated' back to
my cell, I got down on my knees again and said, 'You're
real!' and I could feel the changing power of Jesus take hold
of my body." --
Max Huffman

In the same way, Max was delivered from cursing and his addiction to drugs and alcohol. Through it all, Max had help.
Lay volunteers came into Max's life and discipled him.
Christian friends of Max's wife wrote letters to him and
prayed for him. Max studied bible correspondence courses,
and he grew in the Lord. Even though I had never personally
ministered to Max, I was thrilled and touched to hear that lay
ministry, in all its forms, had assisted Max in finding his place
in God's will.

Looking at Max's wife and child, and seeing the look of joy and peace on their faces, I saw Max in context. I had seen inmates repent, I had seen inmates reform, but his was the first time I had seen an inmate restored. God restored Max to his family and to gainful employment, as well as giving him a ministry to inmates.

Psalm 51:13 reads, "Restore unto me the joy of thy salvation; and uphold me with thy free spirit."

Changed lives, repentance, reformation and restoration: that's what ministry is really all about.

Yes, it's really worth the trip.

If you have been considering jail and prison ministry, I hope this book has been helpful to you in making that decision. If you have decided that jail and prison ministry is not for you, I pray that you find your place in God's will soon. Time is short. May God bless you.

"Then saith he unto his disciples, 'The harvest truly is plenteous, but the laborers are few; Pray ye therefore the Lord of the harvest, that he will send forth laborers into his harvest.'"
Matthew 9:37, 38.

Yours in Christ's Service,
Larry Nielsen

<u>PDF to Word</u>

Made in the USA
Middletown, DE
09 June 2015